I Thought This Was Worth Sharing: Stories and Some Other Stuff About Love and Some Other Stuff

Copyright © 2022 by Scott Muska

All rights reserved. No part of this publication may be reproduced, distributed, or transmitted in any form or by any means, including photocopying, recording, or other electronic or mechanical methods, without the prior written permission of the publisher, except in the case of brief quotations embodied in critical reviews and certain other noncommercial uses permitted by copyright law. For permission requests, write to the publisher, addressed "Attention: Scott Muska," at the address below.

Cover art by Scott Shaffer
www.asyouwishpro.com

Kristen Giuliano
www.giulianodesignco.com

Fourth Bar Books
1060 Bannock St.
Suite 200
Denver, CO 80204

ISBN-13: 978-1-7375636-3-1

Printed in the United States of America

First Edition

14 13 12 11 10 / 10 9 8 7 6 5 4 3 2 1

I Thought This Was Worth Sharing: Stories and Some Other Stuff About Love and Some Other Stuff

By Scott Muska

Throughout this book, names, dates, places, events and certain details have been intentionally changed, mostly to protect the privacy of people I once did or still do care about. If you decide to read any of the pages to come, thank you so much, and I hope you enjoy them.

"It's funny to think about the things in your life that can make you cry just knowing that they existed, can then become the same thing that can make you cry knowing that they're now gone. I think those things come into our lives to help us get from one place to a better one."

— Ted Lasso

"When I'm alone, you're all I think about. But I'm never alone very long."

— Conor Oberst

"Bro, you have no chill."

— An ex-girlfriend

"Buy the ticket, take the ride."

— Hunter S. Thompson

Kindergarten Crush

Several Things I Almost Said the Time a Woman Handed Me a Magnum Condom

Kissing Styles

Rejected Ideas for My Dating App Profile Bios

A First Date

Questions I Don't Have the Fortitude to Ask on a First Date

Neurotic Fiction: Cancelling Plans

Failed Dating App First Lines

Excerpts From My Forthcoming Food-Based Erotica Short Story Collection

Missed Connection: A Lack of Love in a Time of Isolation

Thoughts I've Had While Waiting for Her to Text Back

Why I Haven't Texted You Back

Daiquiris and an Uber Pool Incident

Without Her: Ordering Chinese

Selected Excerpts From Dating Application Cover Letters

Free Stuff: Three-pack (One Opened) of Mrs. Meyers's Clean Day Hand Soap, Geranium Scent

Questions From a Dating Exit Interview

Quiz: Text From Someone I'm Dating or From My Food Delivery Driver?

When You Know They're Fading

Text Messages You Should Probably Not Send As a First Date Follow-Up

Losing My Lip Balm

Reading in Bed, Forever Ago

Reasons They Can't (or Don't Want to) Sleep Over

Some Potential Reasons Why They Ghosted You

1. Kindergarten Crush

Kaitlin was the first girl I ever fell in love with.

I was six, in that stage when you're mostly unaware of the way people you gravitate toward for one reason or another can truly make you feel—so I had no idea what was going on, let alone what I was supposed to call these emotions or how I was supposed to deal with or act on them.

Why did I want to commit the forbidden infraction of jumping off a swing at its peak height during recess to get Kaitlin to pay attention to me, even if just for a few seconds? Why did I want to draw a picture to give her, but ultimately decide not to on account of the inarguable fact that my visual art skills were nowhere near her level and I didn't want to embarrass myself? Why did my stomach feel all kinds of weird, but not in a necessarily bad way, every single time she was within a 10-foot radius?

Again, I was six. I knew nothing of love.

I hadn't come to kindergarten expecting to have to deal with this type of shit.

Not that it was a bad thing, exactly. A good problem to have, as it were. I mean, it was the first time getting to see a girl would actually make me look forward to going to school, even if said girl definitely, if unwittingly, distracted me from my fancy book learnin'.

It would've been kind of nice to go through that "Girls have cooties so keep them far away from me and my toys" phase, though. I think I would have benefited from that kind of stress-free life.

Probably still could.

Kaitlin was talkative, kind and rambunctious, one of the girls who didn't shy away from playing games with the boys during recess. She was definitely faster than me. Probably a better jungle gym climber too. She was an ace with a 24-pack of crayons—winning an art competition that scored her a gift certificate to Variety Basket, a store in our small town where I used to go with my Grandpap when he would pick me up for lunch dates after the half-days of kindergarten. They had all kinds of cool stuff there, but I was drawn to the rings. I've always been into accessories. Especially the cheap kind. (I'm not very classy.)

I mostly kept my distance from Kaitlin. I had no trouble talking with girls I wasn't in like with, but with her I couldn't imagine how to have a normal conversation without coming off like an idiot at best, or crying and peeing my pants at worst.

I Thought This Was Worth Sharing

Adding to my anxiety: I was worried about what the future held for Kaitlin and me. At the end of the kindergarten year, I was unlikely to see her again. My family lived in an ultra-rural area of an already rural school district, which meant I had to attend a tiny, old, decrepit, non-air-conditioned, asbestos-addled elementary school on the outskirts of civilization. It was so small, it didn't even *have* kindergarten, which was why I'd been shipped via short bus throughout that year to one of the district's bigger elementary schools.

But following kindergarten, it would be back to the boondocks while Kaitlin studied miles away. Her family lived in the budding western-Pennsylvania metropolis of Saxonburg, within walking distance of the school, the town's independent video rental store and the aforementioned Variety Basket. She would be staying put post-kindergarten, and besides, she was going to be one of the "gifted" kids, so she had to be at the bigger, nicer school. That kind of curriculum wasn't offered to the riffraff at Clinton Elementary, where I was doomed to spend my days.

Spurred by geographic urgency, I began telling myself at the beginning of every day that that day would be the day—the day I would talk to Kaitlin about something significant, or at least about something insignificant for a significant length of time. Then, at the end of that day, after failing to execute my plan, I would tell myself I had tomorrow and could do something to distinguish myself then. Maybe I'd write her a note, make fun of her at recess (a surprisingly effective maneuver in those days) or, I don't know, just talk to her about horses or coloring. (Horses were a big hit among the girls I grew up with.)

I did this and did this and did this, and then eventually it was the last day of school and I had done, well, nothing. I was ready to resign myself to a summer's worth of moping around, lamenting the fact that I hadn't even fully had love and had still managed to lose it.

But then fate or something like it intervened.

At recess, the ring Kaitlin had purchased at the Variety Basket with her gift certificate fell off her finger during a vigorous game of Freeze Tag. An unfortunate casualty, but one I immediately realized I had the chance to benefit from if I summoned the strength to be some kind of noble, valiant and bold. (I've always been garbage.)

I cast my usual nerves aside and went to work, rallying the search for the missing piece of jewelry like an old-timey general.

I found the ring near the swings.

It was ruined, crushed by a classmate who hadn't seen it lying there, shining like tinfoil in the mulch, and had stepped on it while being chased.

Nonetheless, I solemnly presented the warped and ruined accessory to Kaitlin.

She cried a little but quickly recovered, handling the situation far better than I would have. If my ring had been smashed beyond repair or recognition, I would've been devastated to the point of outwardly showing emotion, likely through a copious amount of tears, something that was discouraged by my parents and pretty much everyone else back then. (In case this isn't already clear, I was a sensitive kid.)

I spent the rest of that last day of school comforting Kaitlin in my six-year-old way, checking on her when I could and telling her I understood how she felt. (I'd had a dropped ring stepped on while traveling on the short bus a couple months before, and it still stung.) All along, I was asking myself why I hadn't done this sooner, this whole speaking-with-her thing. It wasn't so bad, or so difficult. And it probably would have been even easier had I sacked up and started a conversation when she was in a *good* mood.

So now I was sad that Kaitlin was sad, but I was also sad that I'd only started talking to her when the end was nigh. In mere hours, we'd go our separate ways and I'd spend the summer wondering, what if?

I made a quick decision.

Much later, I would realize this was my first ever Grand Romantic Gesture.

I took my ring off my finger and slid it across the table to Kaitlin.

She picked it up, stared at it for a moment and then mouthed, "For me?"

I nodded, nonchalant. Cool as a motherfucker.

She smiled.

We both turned red.

Then she walked out of the room, gone forever.

***

Just kidding.

That summer, my family joined a local pool. This pool turned out to also be Kaitlin's pool, and I started seeing her a few days a week. Then, when I started Sunday School the next year, she was in my class.

And then it happened.

Finally.

At age 11, during the fifth grade: a torrid like affair.

I'd been holding a candle for Kaitlin close to my heart for all these years, and she had finally developed a reciprocal crush on me. This may or may not have had to do with the fact that I'd gotten braces the year before that had worked my teeth into almost normal shape and considerably upped my confidence and my game. I don't want to say Kaitlin was superficial like that, but if you saw photographs of me before and after mouth metal, you might understand my suspicion.

Through a series of AOL Instant Messenger chats with both Kaitlin and her older sister, I found that she was in like with me as well. We flirted via the written word for a little bit and then, just after unceremoniously breaking things off with another girl (like I said, I've always been garbage), I asked Kaitlin to be my girlfriend.

It didn't work out. I dumped her, too, for another girl. I was some sort of budding wannabe lothario. Maybe my parents springing for my braces had been great for my smile and bravado, but horrible for character building.

I guess I, just like so many of us, just liked being wanted. Sometimes I still do.

But things often turn out the way they should, I suppose. Fifteen years after that memorable day in kindergarten, I danced with Kaitlin at her wedding. She remains happily married and has a lovely family.

I remain single and still prone to lackluster Grand Romantic Gestures—sometimes still ones that come in the wake of something being irrevocably broken. Results have varied.

2. Several Things I Almost Said the Time a Woman Handed Me a Magnum Condom

"This'll be like putting a garbage bag on a toothpick."

"This'll be like putting a crew sock on a paper clip."

"This'll be like putting a tube sock on anything."

"I think we need to manage some expectations."

"If I wash this first, will it shrink?"

"We're about to play Just the Reservoir Tip, aren't we?"

[Maniacal laughter.] "Oh, you're not joking?"

"Honestly, look at it, this is as big as it gets. I don't know what you were expecting given my stature and the several jokes I have made via text about how small my penis is."

"Does it come in a smaller size?"

"Can *I* come in a smaller size?"

"To think that would snugly fit my pipe is, in and of itself, a pipe dream."

"Cool! The JNCO Jeans of condoms!"

"Wait. People actually fuck with these? I thought they were made to inflate and hit around crowds at music festivals."

"I have lost all confidence in how I will measure up to partners from your sexual past. Literally."

"Ha! The end of this is going to look like an accordion."

"I'm going to the bodega to find a better fit."

3. Kissing Styles

I would never say you were a bad kisser. Just like I would never say I was a good kisser. It's not like I'm in line to win any awards. I'm sure people from my past would call me a lackluster kisser, and others would corroborate as much.

(I'm sure people from my past would call me at least lackluster about a lot of stuff, and would say that was their way of putting it mildly.)

I don't actually buy the idea that bad kissers are a thing (all kisses are good kisses and good kisses are great kisses or something like that)—though, like with anything, there are certainly exceptions. For example, one night I was on a first date with a woman who seemed more interested in planting her lips and copious amounts of tongue anywhere in the general vicinity of my mandible except for on or in my actual mouth. I think she even spent more time salivating on my neck beard than on where you're supposed to actually kiss. She was not at all happy when I declined to go home with her, and she left me many voice messages in a two-hour span reminding me of what I was missing out on.

My hypothesis is that it's more about stylistic differences than about one or both parties being "bad" at the act of kissing. You know—issues with compatibility, basically. Sometimes you're just not the right fit. Maybe you like to tilt your head one way while they prefer the other, and you battle back and forth, swiveling your necks in a strange (mostly) mouth-to-mouth struggle. Maybe you prefer more tongue than the other person or would prefer a slight shuffle in syncopation that your potential partner just can't seem to nail down.

Maybe you wish this person would just lightly bite your fucking lip a little bit, for once, because that can be fun, right?

Maybe it's another of innumerable intangible differences in approach, duration, etc. Take your pick.

There are countless styles, I'm sure, and sometimes I think people can change said styles; they both can adapt, make somewhat subtle shifts in approach so that the experience of making out is most fully enjoyed by both parties. It's also a thing I think requires some sort of practice.

There was this girl I was with in high school, and we both seemed to get better the more we did it. We learned from and with each other. I still miss her sometimes.

Additionally, I think it's a thing where when you experience someone who really meshes well with whatever your style is, someone you might drunkenly text sometimes to say stuff like, "You're a really good

I Thought This Was Worth Sharing

kisser," well, you start to compare other peoples' kisses to theirs. Your recollection of their lips becomes some kind of litmus test.

So anyway, I don't think we're Kissing Compatible, and I don't think that's going to change. I want to believe we've both been trying to adapt for a while, or at least I have. (Have you noticed that? I've been trying some new tongue stuff that slightly mimics what you seem to be into doing to me. It just feels off somehow, though, like I'm playing a part that wasn't at all meant for me.) Though I don't know for sure if you've been trying to troubleshoot this or if you even see any trouble to begin with.

They say sometimes opposites attract, but I don't think this is one of those times.

And so I think we should call it quits. I mean, think about it: Kissing is crucial. It's instrumental to most relationships, especially in the beginning stages, when you find yourself making out all the time, and if you can't get the kissing down, I don't really know how you make things last.

I don't want to try to change you, and to be honest, I'm kind of cool in my kissing comfort zone. I've grown used to the way I do things, almost attached, you know?

I'm sorry, but I do feel strongly about this. And no, it's not *just* about the kissing.

Oh. You've been seeing someone else and they've just asked you to be exclusive? He's a better kisser? And a much better fit for you all around than me? He's also better at oral?

Well, shit. Way to kick a man about how he goes down.

We probably shouldn't kiss goodbye.

Should we, though? Maybe one last shot? Now I want to prove myself.

Never mind. You're right. That's a stupid idea.

What's done is done. But when were you going to bring this up?

4. Rejected Ideas for My Dating App Profile Bios

I'm like a boxed Shiraz: full-bodied, approachable and occasionally thirst-inducing.

I'm kind of like port wine cheese: soft and not everybody likes me.

I have been so wrong so many times I have swiped right.

Take me to a Chinese buffet and tell me I'm pretty.

Crying on the inside is my default mode.

A woman I recently exchanged messages with on here but never met in real life called me out for not prioritizing dating (which is harsh but not untrue). Then she went on to say that of the past three men she'd dated, one was not yet over his ex, the second worked late too often and the third was going through a bout of depression—none of which she was down with. So, in the interest of transparency, I feel like I should let you know that I am not fully over my ex, I often work a lot of hours and I am very prone to bouts of depression.

I'm like the offspring of a VSCO girl and a broken McFlurry machine.

In the past decade, I've eaten the vast majority of my meals off a coffee table. I'm hoping you can help me change that.

I'm just here on the apps patiently awaiting the first wave of divorces in my age range.

I've never been "love-at-first-sight" material, but if you give me a chance, there's maybe potential that I will grow on you—though not like a fungal infection or anything like that.

What if these platforms exist just to beat us down until we finally make peace with the notion that maybe we've had unrealistic expectations and standards all along? That the league we see ourselves in is actually way out of our league?

I'd almost always rather be on the couch.

What if "The One" doesn't exist? And if "The One" does exist, what am I supposed to do when they inevitably exit?

An ex once told me I can't commit to a pair of socks. And she's right. I almost never wear socks.

I have to be blackout drunk to dance. And I dance *a lot.*

I THOUGHT THIS WAS WORTH SHARING

What brings me to the apps? Well, one time I thought I had met the girl of my dreams, but she ended up being the woman of my night terrors.

I'm a workaholic, but that might not be a bad thing, because I'm told that relationships take hard work.

I'd pick you up for our first date, but I don't have a car.

I'm very organized. I keep this and several other dating apps in a neat folder on my phone titled "Don't Die Alone."

I'm melodramatic but never mellow. I sweat profusely because I have no chill.

I've never believed in the three-day rule as it applies to both asking for a second date and consuming leftovers.

This is one of the places I spend my time when I'm not poring over my ex's Instagram.

I'm just here because my missed connection posts weren't working out.

I'm so single, I often worry that I'll stay that way and run out of mediocre sitcoms to binge-watch alone.

My Patronus is Eeyore. Or out-of-shape David Harbour.

What's the most recent thing you googled? Mine's "Do I have a fear of intimacy?"

Swipe left if you don't know what anhedonia is.

I wish I could afford to take you out to a nicer place, but I spend a lot of my money on therapy because my psychologist is out of network.

I'm a complete mess, but my apartment is mostly clean.

Know any good photographers? I need some new images for this thing.

I'm made up mostly of MSG, Mountain Dew and fear.

I live for the nights I won't remember with the carbs I'll never regret.

In any given day, I generally receive more push notifications from Domino's than from this app. Speaking of pizza, I'm open to relocation because I'll go anywhere for love, and also because Little Caesars recently started delivering but not within my zip code.

Sometimes it feels like I wouldn't even match with water if I fell out of a fucking boat.

I don't really have the time or energy to craft an opening message that is more creative than a simple inquiry into your weekend plans. So maybe I don't have the time or energy to be dating, now that I really think about it.

I'm currently in what you might call a "rebuilding phase." Have been since 1987.

I'm (kind of) a man in his early 30s who still sleeps with stuffed animals and the blanket he got the day he was born. And I occasionally anthropomorphize them. Figured I'd get that out of the way now because if you ever came over to my place and didn't know, I'd feel compelled to hide them. Then one day I'd inevitably forget, and then

I Thought This Was Worth Sharing

you'd know, and it might even weirder than me just coming straight out with it. Also, I am a Scorpio.

I was in love once. I just didn't know it at the time.

You better not let me get hot! Because that probably means I'm having yet another gout flare-up.

I don't really like to exercise all that much anymore, but I tell you what: I will *sprint* away from intimacy and commitment!

I guess I'd say that one thing that makes me unique is that I don't have a podcast.

I'm actually not all that huge on traveling (probably mostly because I have nobody to travel with, hence my being on this app), but boy, I would really love to take a vacation from myself.

I can't help you build shit or put things together but I *can* navigate the TaskRabbit app, so the end result will be the same.

I could probably win an award for creative self-sabotage.

I haven't had a significant falling out in a while, unless you count the one with my hair. I'm just a dude with a comb-over looking for a do-over.

I used to be good at sports back in high school.

Scott Muska

5. A First Date

I showed up sweating. This was not a surprise to me. Sweating is a calling card—a big part of my personal brand, unfortunately—and the fact that I was meeting a stranger *and* sweating and thinking about how I was sweating? This didn't help the sweating.

Our first drink helped calm the nerves, and by the time we were nearing the end of the round, my sweating had mostly subsided. Things were, by my standards, "going well."

The conversation was friendly and flowing, revolving around a mutual admiration of the extremely absurd music video for the Celine Dion classic "It's All Coming Back to Me Now." We ordered another round of specialty cocktails. I took a sip of mine and it tasted mostly like whiskey.

I love whiskey and also have an unrefined palate when it comes to whiskey, so pretty much the only comment I could muster about the drink was, "This is pretty good!"

She took a sip of hers. I asked how it was.

She wrinkled her brow, then grinned.

"It tastes like semen," she said. "Want a sip?"

Following a silence bordering on the uncomfortable, I shook my head no.

"But it tastes like semen!"

"Exactly," I said. With finality, I thought.

"So?"

"I don't want to taste something that tastes like semen."

"Have you never tasted semen?"

"I have not."

"You seriously haven't fucking tried it?"

"Nope."

And here's the thing: I didn't really want to taste any semen. I've had plenty of people tell me that semen is not a tasty treat. (A few have told me it's not that bad or that they enjoy it, but in this case, at least for me, the majority rules.)

I Thought This Was Worth Sharing

She followed this up with a diatribe about how amazed she was that I'd never gotten curious and taken a lick of my own ejaculate, or that I'd never experimented with another man and tasted his. Maybe I'm not progressive or lack curiosity in that arena, but the closest I've ever gotten is to smell it, unless there has been some in a post-fellatio kiss. And neither scenario was *awesome* for me, so going a step further to intentionally lick it is something that has never occurred to me. I'm not going to yuck anyone's yum here, as I know I'm fully aware I may be coming off as a prude, and more power to you if you do dig the taste, but my personal preference is to Irish Spring it on down the drain.

She dropped the topic in favor of another: She said she liked to ask obscure questions on first dates and then asked me which part of a human baby I would eat first if I was going to eat a human baby.

"I'd go with one of their meaty little thighs," she said with a slightly sinister laugh that made me believe she might have entertained the notion of actually doing such a thing.

I told her I was a pescatarian. Which I wasn't and am not. But in that moment, it was a lie I was more than comfortable with.

"But if you weren't, though," she said.

"I just...I don't want to think about eating a baby," I said and then changed the subject to something like what she did for work or where she grew up.

Luckily, she didn't press the issue. But I'd be lying if I said, weirded out as I was, that I didn't start to consider what my answer might be. I really like the idea of asking atypical questions on a first date that go further than the run-of-the-mill conversations I'm used to, and I respected her for really going for it. I have many things I'd like to ask women the first time we meet, but I tend to bite my tongue due to lack of testicular fortitude mixed with the illusion of decorum, and I felt kind of guilty for not playing ball with someone who had no issue whatsoever with really pushing the boundaries of normalcy, beyond the pale as her question might've been.

I felt like things were no longer going quite as well due to my refusal to fully participate in her hopefully theoretical dialogue idea, but we still kissed good night at the end of the date because, well, buy the ticket, take the ride.

Then, just before she turned away to walk in the opposite direction, she said, "Before we see each other again, you should totally sample your semen!"

I laughed a nervous laugh. This was hands down the strangest way anyone had ever expressed interest in seeing me again after a first date—especially considering the vibe I had to have been giving off.

When I got back to my Bushwick apartment, I debriefed my roommate and one of our friends who was over to play video games.

At the semen part, our friend paused the game, looked at me with incredulity and said, "You've never tasted your own semen?"

"No!"

"Really?"

"You have?"

"Fucking weirdo," he said, then shook his head and went back to the game. My roommate remained silent during the exchange, which led

I THOUGHT THIS WAS WORTH SHARING

me to believe he'd tried semen before and that I really was some sort of outlier.

To this day I have not tried my own semen, but I'm not going to rule it out. It seems like the older I get, the weirder things become.

Scott Muska

6. Questions I Don't Have the Fortitude to Ask on a First Date

So, what do you do...when you find yourself in the grip of a crippling existential crisis?

What would your stage name be if you were a rapper? And keep in mind that you can't choose 2 Chinz because I've already called dibs.

What if we really connected and hit it off tonight and then got serious, but I eventually went bald? Would this bother you nearly as much as it would bother me?

What're your views on copious amounts of chest hair? Like, almost long enough to braid and, if left to its own devices, will grow high enough on the body to seamlessly connect with a neck beard?

Are you someone who likes to cuddle while sleeping? If so, do you find it off-putting to wake up in a puddle of your spooner's sweat? And since we're on the topic of slumber, what are your views on not sleeping with your serious significant other or spouse on a nightly basis if said significant other happens to be better at sleeping on their own, usually in borderline freezing temperatures?

How many times in the past fiscal quarter have you done something specifically to post it on social media and not because it was something you felt like you wanted to do? Did you feel a dopamine spike with each incoming like?

Have you ever found yourself in a position (as it were) where a safe word was warranted? If so, what was yours? Do you wish you'd gotten more creative with it?

How much boxed red wine would you say is too much?

Do I appear too drunk right now?

How much does not wanting your potential offspring to inherit certain traits, tendencies, illnesses or aspects of your inherent temperament or personality contribute to where you stand on whether or not you would like to be a biological parent someday?

Are you the kind of person who needs alone time every once in a while to recharge? Can you empathize with someone who is, or at least sympathize? Will you be upset if things progress and I sometimes have to spend days and nights by myself? Do you realize that these are the kinds of questions I have to ask up front because my need for solitude has been a contentious issue in the past, to the point that it was a dealbreaker, which is kind of sad but also something I totally understand?

I THOUGHT THIS WAS WORTH SHARING

Do you happen to have any great remedies to help alleviate eczema that shows up often on the back, occasionally on the face and sometimes on the penis?

If I were to lend you a book and then we decided to go our separate ways while you still had that book, what would you do with the book?

Do you believe it is OK to tell lies or untruths if nobody is likely going to get hurt and it is, in your realistically earnest opinion, for "the greater good"?

What is your favorite thing to do when you're procrastinating at your place of employment?

Say a musician unwittingly comes up with a song that relieves all anxiety immediately. And it can do so forever, if listened to once a day at the exact same time (down to the minute). If you miss a day, however, you will be addled for one full year with the same level of anxiety you used to experience until listening to the song will resume having a positive effect on your thoughts and moods. Do you listen to this song for the first time?

What do you do when you're doing nothing?

You've found someone who is perfect for you in every way except when it comes to sexual chemistry. Aside from that, you can see yourself building a life together with them, growing old together, starting a family if that's something you both want to do, etc. But you also somehow know for certain that the sex is never going to get that much better, regardless of how much you communicate or what you try. Do you continue to date this person?

What is the ideal job or vocation that your mate could have? How important is that sort of thing to you, and how much does (or how much do you allow) your job to define your identity?

Mirrors and reflections suddenly completely cease to exist. Is this a good or bad thing? Do you ever think about how much time you spend looking at your own reflection?

You somehow find out that you are going to die and that many of your organs will be viable for donation. However, you also find out that at least some of them will go to some terrible, terrible people. There's no guarantee that some of them won't go to great, more-than-deserving people, though. Do you take measures to no longer be an organ donor, or do you allow your organs to be donated? Also, if you aren't currently an organ donor, what the fuck?

Why is your birthday important?

Someone you really took a liking to sends you a message months after disappearing without communication, let alone explanation, following three dates. How do you respond, if you respond at all?

If aliens showed up on Earth tomorrow (like, blatantly, to a point where their existence would no longer be somewhat hidden like it almost definitely is right now) to completely decimate human civilization, does this rule out any belief you may currently have in god? And if you don't currently believe in god, how important is it that your partner in a long-term relationship share your belief in disbelief?

Do you ever think about how strange it is that we spend so much time pursuing orgasms when they last mere seconds?

What would you want engraved on your headstone?

When you wake up in the middle of the night, what keeps you from fall-

I Thought This Was Worth Sharing

37

ing back to sleep? What thoughts creep in when you're semi-conscious and in the middle of that piss you take before returning to your bed?

Let's imagine my favorite band is Nickelback. Is that going to be a problem? Do you hate the band like so many others do even though they've probably done more good than bad for the world, if you really think about it? (Like, they have probably saved lives, and I don't say that melodramatically. Music is powerful.) Would you be willing to admit that some of their songs are objectively not *that bad* and that a lot of distaste for the band is a result of groupthink?

A zombie apocalypse begins. Does any part of you (strange as it sounds) feel some sort of relief, because now you will only (theoretically) be worrying about, like, surviving, and you won't ever have to worry about petty shit again because you won't really have the bandwidth to do so because you'll be spending all your time trying not to get fucking bitten and/or annihilated? Do you think something like this would bring out the best or worst in most of the people you know best?

It is confirmed that we are indeed living in a simulation. How does this make you feel?

If heaven exists in some form, how do you think we show up there? What age are we? Is it the age we're at when we die, or the age we're at when we hit our peak? Or is everyone in heaven just the same age? Do we age at all while there? Do we get some say in all this? What about in hell, if that too exists?

Do you agree that in some situations, ghosting is completely appropriate? If so, what scenarios might warrant it? And would you be willing to accept being ghosted in said scenarios?

Do you ever google yourself? If so, do you like what you find?

Do you believe in defining the relationship, or do you think people tend to reach a point in a relationship when they tacitly become a couple?

How are you really doing?

7. Neurotic Fiction: Cancelling Plans

When she asks if you want to order dinner, you're a bit taken aback. It's a question you weren't expecting. A drink, sure, but a full meal? On a Friday night?

***

Generally, you try not to propose dinner on a first date. It seems too soon, too intimate, to eat in front of someone else. One time, and this was a while back, you *did* eat something on a first date, caution to the wind and all that, only to discover when you went to the restroom nearly 20 minutes after finishing your food that you had a red sauce stain on the side of your mouth shaped like the state of Kentucky.

You found out later on that you'd drizzled a little bit onto your shirt as well. Why the fuck'd you get red sauce? Because you were more-than-slightly unsettled, having just met a new person you might one day kiss (that day, even!) if things went a certain way, and you panic-ordered, that's why. You didn't even have an appetite, but what were you supposed to do? Just sit there and watch your date eat? That'd be the weirdest possible type of inaction.

***

"I will absolutely go on this date tonight," you tell yourself. "Even if it's not great, I will at least have done it. It's time for me to get back out there. The ex has. I've seen it on Instagram. I've seen it a lot—though, to be fair, I've checked her profile a lot—and no matter what happens, it will be better than spending another Friday night at home alone. Probably."

You admit to yourself, with some hesitance, that spending your recreational time alone over the weekend evenings is better than it could be, but potentially not as good as it should be.

There's a plan you have in place for before the actual agreed-upon date plans, a pre-plan plan, which you hope will help quell the anxiety you've been feeling about this whole thing since you first matched. It's a before-the-date drink at a bar next door that has a two-for-one happy hour. A double rail scotch should, in theory, help calm the nerves.

***

To give yourself enough time for this (kind of unsettling but equally understandable) indulgence, you arrived at the office nice and early that morning, about an hour before everyone else, because you knew you might need to get a head start on the day if you stood any chance of leaving in time to get those drinks in.

I Thought This Was Worth Sharing

That didn't work out.

"Where do you want to get it from? The food? Your choice," she says. "I'm flexible and not really in any kind of particular mood. Though I could eat a salad. But I could also eat something bad for me. I mean, it's a Friday night, so whatever. You know what? Fuck salad."

"Yeah. Fuck salad," you say. "Order whatever. I don't even care."

The internal check-in on the project that had to be done yesterday (everything always has to be done yesterday) didn't go so well, and now you're stuck late. At the office. While others frolic off into their weekend. Their dates. Their fun. Their families. (You've occasionally thought of making up a family just so you'd have a slew of fake obligations that would serve as excuses to leave the office at a normal hour. You've even considered doctoring some photos of a fake clan to keep at your desk and making up some backstories about each member's hobbies and interests.)

Instead of drinks with a semi-stranger, you'll be dining with your project and account managers, the people you already spend most of your waking life with.

You pull out your phone to text that you can't make it and that you would love to reschedule, most of you hoping she will understand and be amenable to it.

But then there's a part of you that's feeling some sense of relief right now—and that same part of you knows you'll be just as angst-addled as you are this time ahead of the next time you make plans, if indeed there is one.

Maybe it'll just be easier to not meet this person ever, to wonder what could have been instead of actually finding out what it's like to have it all crash and burn at some point, which you've been conditioned (or conditioned yourself) to believe is the inevitable conclusion to any attempt at a relationship.

"It probably won't work out anyway," you tell yourself, like you always tell yourself.

"So I'm the worst, but..." you begin to type out.

***

You never really know what's happening on the other end of things, though.

At least not until you've dated for a while. And sometimes not even then.

"You bet your sweet ass you gotta work late," she whispers when the text message notification comes through—just as she's about to finish the first of what might be two (but almost definitely no more than two because holy shit keep it together it's just a date) pre-date in-office drinks. "Hell fucking yeah you hope we can reschedule."

She waits a few minutes before responding to elevate suspense and feign disappointment, choosing instead to begin the commute home-ward and text you somewhere around the halfway point. It's rather uncouth for one to let on that they're fine with a cancellation, even when they are in fact at least partially looking forward to not going on the date they thought they would be going on. When she woke that morning, she was stricken with an undesired *want* to just, you know, finish work for the week and go the fuck home. There would be plenty of other nights available for attempting to find lasting love.

I THOUGHT THIS WAS WORTH SHARING

But her friends tell her she should date more, should get better at getting out there. It's just sometimes she just doesn't feel so much like socializing.

"You're not the worst," she begins to type. "I've had a hell of a week too ..."

***

You finally arrive home, where you order the peel-and-eat shrimp and pour a glass of cheap Malbec, something you do only in private because yikes, seafood with a red, you goddamn maniac? You've decided to order more food despite having already eaten at the office because fuck it, it's Friday, so why not fourth-meal it to begin your weekend?

***

She got home a few hours earlier than you, ordered the double-fried pork belly and coupled it with a couple of pale ales from a microbrewery her friend wouldn't shut the hell up about. A six-pack had caught her eye at the local bodega.

***

You suit up in your nightwear (you're not going to keep your work clothes on for couch and bed time, because imagine where those things have been all day) and queue up *The X-Files*. Even with as hectic a schedule as you have, you've somehow managed to plow through about half the episodes of the series. For the third time. You're still not entirely convinced that the truth is out there, but you still do want to believe.

***

She took off her office-casual clothing and put on *The Office*. Even though she'd already seen every episode of the best seasons at least four times each.

***

You text again, first apologizing for the semi-late hour. You tell her you hope she had a great evening and you're finally home from work (even though she didn't ask for any sort of update on that front).

***

She texts back with her third "No worries" of the night and a slight fib about having met friends out, then signs off by saying she looks forward to making new plans once the two of you have an idea of what next week's hectic schedules will be like.

***

You sigh, happy that you will, after all, be able to meet this person. Just some other time. Allegedly. And you promise yourself that even if work tries to get in the way, you won't let it. Because if you don't meet them, no matter how anxious the initial meeting might make you, then you'll never really know if things could have worked out.

"Next time, I'll be ready," you say to no one, still somewhat confident in the notion that there will always be a next time until things work out for you and there won't have to be.

***

So you went on a first date on a Friday night.

I THOUGHT THIS WAS WORTH SHARING

You even had dinner.

Alone, together. Or together, alone.

Scott Muska

8. Failed Dating App First Lines

Maybe we'll start messaging on here and then go out and hit it off and end up together for all time? You could be my "Forever Wedding Date"! Which would definitely be a step up, as my current one is a marijuana vape pen.

How's your week going?

What are your views on salad? Because I just spent the entire time it took me to consume a salad thinking about what kind of junk I'm going to eat tonight to offset my responsible and non-gluttonous lunch choice. I'm the kind of guy who believes in balance.

Hey.

I was reading your profile and I think it's pretty cool you're the person at the party who can be found hanging out with all the dogs. Maybe someday you can come over to my place and meet my pets. I hope you have a decent imagination, though, because they are stuffed animals.

I bet you like avocados and sarcasm.

Would you like to get naked and start a revolution?

Those are some cool beach pictures! I've been to the coast before as well. I thought it was pretty fine. I will say, though, that I'm mostly ambivalent about long walks on the beach. I would take one with you if that was what you really wanted to do, but I'm more into, like, moderate mileage when it comes to strolling by the sea. Not that it's not picturesque, but sand isn't the easiest to walk on. Also, have you ever seriously thought about how completely frightening and intimidating the ocean is? It could end us all at any time, and there might be some nefarious beings living down there, waiting to come to the surface and wreak supreme havoc.

Your profile is like the 87th I've come across this week that emphatically lists how much you love to travel. So this is the 87th message I'm sending this week confirming that I, too, enjoy traveling whenever I have the chance. Wanderlust is totally dope!

Hey, sorry, I don't think it's going to work out. I didn't want to be that guy who matched with you and then just never sent you a message, but I impulsively swiped right having only seen your first photo and didn't see the image of you eating pizza with a fork and knife until I got the notification that we matched. It's a dealbreaker for me, to be honest. JUST KIDDING! HA! I wasn't being honest at all. I'm so alone that I pretty much don't believe in dealbreakers anymore. I'd still totally love to get to know you even though you eat pizza like a weirdo. Hope to hear from you!

I Thought This Was Worth Sharing

You ever think about marriage?

What're you doing on Saturday night? Want to hang out and gaze into the abyss together? Unless, of course, a weekend first date violates some kind of rule you have, which is totally understandable.

Sometimes I feel like I'm the unreliable narrator of my own life story. Know what I mean?

Just so you know, my man breasts aren't as large in real life as they look in my photos. It's like the camera adds 10 pounds right in that area on me for some reason. I don't want to show up and unpleasantly surprise you by not looking like I do on the app, and have you be like, "What the hell? I thought this dude had a killer rack." That wouldn't be cool of me.

How was your day? I spent mine brainstorming what tattoo I can get to cover up the one I have that prominently features the name of my ex. Any ideas? I'm definitely open to suggestions.

You're not married, are you? I don't know why I asked. I don't really care if you are or not. I'll wreck a home. I have no scruples.

What have you been up to on this snow day? I've been working on my Boner Jamz playlist.

My friend is getting married in Montenegro next year, and for once I'd like to show up with a plus one. Just throwing that out there.

Hello. I hope this finds you well. I'm looking for someone to love more than I love mayonnaise. I have been on various apps, including this one, for years and have yet to find this level of unconditional adoration.

Scott Muska

9. Excerpts From My Forthcoming Food-Based Erotica Short Story Collection

"Guac's always extra," he said, winking as he rubbed mashed avocado and cilantro all over his naked body. "It has that good fat. Look at me: I'm a big, bad walking taco."

"Good morning," he whispered as he poured maple syrup all over his chest. "I'm the most important meal of the day."

"We accept the love we think we deserve," he whispered as he prepared to place his order from the street meat cart, including extra white sauce, but on the side.

"Go ahead," he said. "Treat me like a piece of meat." He handed me a bottle of A1 steak sauce and a dry rub.

"No, no, no—*I'm* the best part of waking up," he whispered as he began to dump a carafe of cold brew over his head while maintaining intense eye contact. When he'd poured out every last drop, he pointed to his genitals and said, "Do you take yours with nut milk?"

"My safe word is *vegan*."

Just before he walked out the door, he turned around and said with a sigh, "Of all the things we lose in this life, weight is one of the easiest to find." I never saw him again.

"I hear you like to party," he said as he cut up a line of Lipitor on my coffee table. "So let's get weird."

"I'll be right back," he said with a wink. "I'm going to slip into something more comfortable." Five minutes later, he returned. "These are my Domino's Eating Pants," he said. "Do you like the elastic band?"

"You can call me the prison warden," he said. "Because if you stay here with me, you'll always get three hots and a cot."

"I don't know if you can keep up with me," he whispered. "Do you think you can? Because let me tell you something: I live every day like it's cheat day."

"My cholesterol won't go down, but I will," he whispered as he ate an entire string cheese stick in one bite.

"I live my life a Quarter Pounder at a time."

"Vegan. *Vegan.* VEGAN!"

10. Missed Connection: A Lack of Love in a Time of Isolation

I was at home alone.

Passing the days.

Not really living.

Just killing time.

Listening to way too much Radiohead.

Taking some liberties with my ramen recipes.

Building pillow and blanket forts to cocoon in and shit.

Taking care to not use more toilet paper than I absolutely needed when, well, taking a shit.

Talking to my stuffed animals like they were people.

At one point asking them if they thought they were better'n me.

Going down to my lobby to get the mail and feeling like a fucking extrovert.

Waiting for the next on-screen conference call so I could virtually lay eyes on and interact with other human beings.

Attempting to out-pizza The Hut.

Gaining my Quarantine 15.

(Those two were probably related.)

Putting on pants just to feel alive.

And to make sure they still almost fit.

Considering steaming, then donning, a full suit and tie just to briefly meet my Chinese food delivery guy.

Getting ghosted and wondering if, given the times, asking the offending party something like "Hey, are you legitimately OK?" was appropriate or just creepy and poor form.

Losing whatever semblance of having my shit together that I'd worked maybe medium-hard for.

I Thought This Was Worth Sharing

There was really nowhere else to go but home—no gatherings big or small, as I'm sure you know.

Who doesn't?

You were probably at home alone, too.

At least this is what I assume and have been envisioning.

Or hoping for.

It is not at all lost on me that this—my hope that you were at home alone—is a very strange thing to actively want for someone in most cases.

But it was weird times.

And this was not most cases.

To clarify: I hope you were home alone unless you absolutely had to be out *there*, in the world, physically, which means most likely that you were and still are—no, that you were and are almost *definitely*—doing more important work than I was or am.

That you were essential.

If you were, thank you for doing what you did.

I really don't have any idea where you are.

Or who you are.

I probably never will.

And that's what bothers me.

It keeps me up at night.

I can't even dream about you if it's true that you can't dream about someone you've never seen—and I swear I heard that somewhere.

A global pandemic can certainly bring people closer together, especially people who are in love with each other and not driven negatively wild by being in constantly close proximity for days, weeks, months on end.

But this kind of thing can also really get in the way of love and the potential to find it.

How many chances have we not had while in semi-forced isolation?

How many of us missed out on meeting someone who could have been the love of our life because the only place we felt safe enough to go was from bed to desk to couch to kitchen to bathroom?

Timing is important.

It can define your life.

And it can do so in ways you'll never even know about.

We could have met at some point during our daily commute.

You may have gotten on the same train as me.

We may have locked eyes.

I THOUGHT THIS WAS WORTH SHARING

I might have seen you at a bar or a party or some other gathering and said something corny as hell to myself or my friends, something like "There. There she is. She's the one, at long last."

I may or may not have somehow summoned the strength to approach you and say hi or something.

And if not, that would've been on me, at least.

I'd have something to kick myself about.

But we'll never know, will we?

We'll never have that chance.

I'll always miss you, for the rest of my life maybe, without even having any idea who I'm missing.

Scott Muska

11. Thoughts I've Had While Waiting for Her to Text Back

I'm sure she'll text back soon even though I've thought of roughly a million reasons why she won't text soon or, well, ever again. I suppose the only thing to do here is to revisit every single text message I've sent over the past 72 hours and do a deep dive into the content. A good ole messaging audit. While doing this analysis, I guess I should also concoct every possible worst-case scenario that the aforementioned content could have catalyzed.

Wait. Didn't you just do this like half an hour ago? Why do you keep doing this to yourself? It's not like the things you've done in the past can be changed. What's been said has been said. All you can do now is hope for the best.

But I know I'll continue to assume the worst! And if I never hear back from her, I'll continue to worry for the better part of a year, won't I? And maybe even after a year, I'll occasionally think about her for no good reason. She'll just pop into my mind, and then I'll get that sad pang in my stomach and wonder what happened and why. I'll have some ruminations on things like:

Did I wait too long?

Did I text too soon?

What if something happened to her?

Calm down. Be rational. Things are probably fine.

But what if they aren't? My intrusive catastrophic thoughts have, albeit rarely, been on point before, and once I was right once or twice, I knew I could be right again no matter how improbable the odds or how untrustworthy my worries tend to be.

Call her.

The fuck? No. Definitely not. Now *that* would be crazy. A phone call. Good lord.

I wonder how many other people she's texting. And how much more she likes those people. I wish I could see pictures, maybe learn some pertinent details.

Whatever. She's not that great anyway.

Boy, do I wish I really believed that!

I Thought This Was Worth Sharing

How in the hell did people wait around for other people to return their letters?

Maybe it was easier for them back in the day because they hadn't become trained to expect instant responses because such things were impossible unless they happened to be with someone in person.

This certainly makes me yearn for a simpler time.

Maybe you should follow up.

I should probably follow up. Good call. Wait. No. I should definitely, absolutely not follow up. Because my instincts are telling me to follow up. And no matter what, I should never follow my instincts. They're my enemy. Especially when it comes to anything even tangentially affiliated with romance. Seems counterintuitive because it is, but it's generally just the way it is.

Have it your way. How about you try giving it some time?

I guess I could read a book. Or I could watch a movie. Or do something else I've been putting off that I've been anxious about avoiding.

Good thinking.

No. None of that will work. I'll just keep checking my phone. Oh! I can masturbate! Because I can't touch my phone when my hand is covered in lube! Ha. Who am I kidding? I have two hands. Nothing will stop me from obsessively checking my phone. I even do it when I'm pissing.

Yeah, I mean—try not to lie to yourself. You've long since mastered the art of holding your phone one-handed while queuing up a Bang Bus episode and pounding one down. Remember that time you were visiting

*your parents' house for the holidays and you did just that, then got so into
things that you actually broke their fucking toilet?*

Good point, though I've been trying to forget about that whole thing.
Anyway, I guess this whole dalliance was fun while it lasted. Time to
incessantly beat myself up over what I may have done wrong!

Maybe she's just busy at work.

Maybe she wants me to *think* she's busy at work. I think that's called
playing it coy or some shit.

*Maybe you should entertain the notion that you barely know her and
don't yet deserve to be anywhere too high on her list of priorities? And how
about you just go to bed?*

There is no way I'm sleeping until I hear back from her. Which means,
now that I think about it, I may never sleep again. Ever. Why do I even
try to date? This shit is really not worth it. I should just eat and drink
whatever and whenever I want and get fat and not worry about cou-
pling anymore ever. Who needs the romantic love of another human
when you have unbridled access to delivery Taco Bell? I can Live Más
all by myself.

*That's some real sad-sounding shit, man. Get your act together. Maybe
you should write something. That usually helps you feel better.*

You're right.

But not another text to her, though.

Noted.

I THOUGHT THIS WAS WORTH SHARING

12: Why I Haven't Texted You Back

I fell asleep.

I was driving my team down the field during a pickup flag football game and the drive ultimately ended in a failed two-point attempt that would have knotted things up, so I'm still a little too despondent to text message *anybody*, including my own mother, who texted several hours ago and automatically thinks I have perished in some horrible way every time I don't answer her messages within 15 minutes.

I was driving an actual car.

I don't want to get gravy on my phone. The less you know regarding specifics, the better. Just trust me.

I typed and re-typed a response to you but wanted to focus-group it among friends to bolster my confidence around the notion that I am succinctly yet effectively getting my desired message across. So it's currently in testing. Could be I'm advised to kill the entire correspondence and start from scratch, which will further delay things, but we'll see.

My (stuffed) dog ate my phone. Either that or he hid it so he can find some way to play online poker with it after I go to sleep at night. How he will do this without opposable thumbs or, you know, a beating heart or actual life force of any kind that extends beyond my own imagination, I am not quite sure.

I've begun seeing someone else, and while in her eyes it is still (I think) casual, I would feel guilty "talking" with other people, like I was betraying her in some way, even though that's definitely putting the proverbial cart before the horse or whatever on my end. Fuck. Now I'm wondering if she's been talking to other people too, and if so, how many and how much this should or should not matter. I see that she's added new photos to her online dating profile, so she's definitely still out there. I'll be right back. I gotta go see my psyche about a rabbit hole.

I can't come to the phone right now because I am currently in the midst of a thought-spiral crisis wherein I'm imagining a future that my mind will for some reason allow me to envision only as bleak at best.

I got elbows-deep in a wing-eating contest...with myself. I was a worthy adversary and it required all of my day's focus, grit and determination. There is ranch dressing *everywhere.*

I completely forgot to text you back. I am sorry and hope you're not sitting around waiting for a message from me—which I know is a vain

I THOUGHT THIS WAS WORTH SHARING

statement. I just know that the way I think and operate, I start to freak out when people don't respond to me in what I subjectively deign to be a timely manner. I hope you're not like me, but if you are, I'm sorry for that, too. And in that case, I double-apologize for not having been more attentive and theoretically punctual in answering you.

There's this new thing I'm trying where I check my phone less often and do something productive instead, like breathing exercises, writing in my journal or making myself a meal that is not General Tso's chicken delivered from the Chinese takeout place that I frequent enough that if I didn't order for more than three consecutive days, they would probably send someone to check up on me to make sure I'm OK. (It now occurs to me that I should probably at some point find an emergency contact other than my parents, who live hundreds of miles away. Maybe I'll ask the delivery guy.)

I am high as a kite, and the only thing I can concentrate on at present is the Domino's order tracking app.

I am a complete coward.

I don't really like you all that much and don't feel like I owe you a goddamn thing.

I'm convening with nature—and by that I mean I'm in the park, watching couples and wondering why I'm so alone. And while I don't always like being alone, I'm not convinced you're the person I want to be not alone with, and I don't know just how to tell you that.

Scott Muska

ction
13. Daiquiris and an Uber Pool Incident

We were on our third round of daiquiris, the legit kind, when I told her that this was the first time I'd ever had the real thing. And that they were delicious.

Before this, I'd only ever had the gaudy, frozen variety from trying-too-hard beach-themed bars in landlocked states. They gave me brain freeze instantly and a sugar-induced hangover later.

"This place is known for its daiquiris," she said when she showed up. "So I'm going to have one of those. You should, too. You can get that anywhere," she said, pointing at my glass of Johnnie Walker.

I—a man of habit and blind brand loyalty—bristled at her dismissal of the drink and rocks glass you could often find serving as an extension of my left hand. But then I remembered I'd just been telling myself that liking whiskey isn't necessarily the most unique or compelling personality trait, if it was a personality trait at all.

So I put aside concerns about trying something new for once and about mixing the two forms of booze in my digestive system and followed her lead, which is how we ended up at Daiquiri number three, during which I made my admission and she made her move, telling me she actually made "a pretty mean" daiquiri herself, if I wanted to come to her apartment to try her recipe.

"Anyway, better to get out of this place soon because the later it gets, the more rowdy it gets," she said.

I accepted her invitation and told her I, too, was all about starting early and finishing early—I liked to be home at a decent hour so I could hydrate and watch a recording of that night's *Jeopardy* episode before falling into a fitful slumber.

"Yeah, the thirties are...not quite as wild, are they?" she said. "Oh, and just so you know, this doesn't mean I'm going to sleep with you. I have a three-date rule. My pants stay on until then at the very soonest."

"I wasn't going to make any assumptions one way or the other, but thanks for letting me know up front," I said. "This way I won't even try to shoot my shot. But just remember, you can't sleep with someone if you never spend the night, and I really like sleeping in my own bed."

"Are you actively trying to blow this?"

"I was just kidding. I really would like another daiquiri, though."

"I know. Just wait 'til you get one down the hatch. I make good shit. Let's go."

I Thought This Was Worth Sharing

After the awkward first-date check-settling ritual, she called us an Uber to a liquor store a couple blocks from her place, where we could pick up some rum and limes and whatever other supplies she might need because she couldn't remember exactly what she had in-house.

"Oops," she said while tapping at her phone. "I think I just got us an Uber Pool. I don't want to cancel it and mess with my rating."

"Yeah, don't do that. Maybe we'll meet some interesting strangers anyway."

I knew an Uber rating was sacred. I'd been trying to get mine built back up after it took a dip earlier in the year when I had my first ever gout flare-up. I could barely walk and had to take some embarrassingly short rides to the podiatrist around the corner from my apartment and then to the pharmacy to get some meds. (As I write this years later, I have given up on my Uber rating and have switched fully to Lyft. Sometimes the best way to win is to quit.)

Plus, an Uber Pool, a new offering from the company at the time, was an easy way to save a few bucks, especially if you weren't in any real hurry. Which we weren't. No rush to take pants off. Not this time.

"I hope we're not in a car with weirdos," she said.

"If we are, we can make the most of it."

We left the bar, and while we were waiting for a car to arrive, she told me she sometimes had a tendency to get car sick and that it might be better for her to sit in the front seat.

"Shotgun is yours, for sure," I said.

"We can just pretend we're holding hands in the backseat, though," she said, then took my hand in the street.

I was stunned and a little bit elated, but also worried that my hands were sweaty. Holding hands is an intimate thing if you think about it, especially if you think too much about it, which I did, but I was mostly glad we were taking such a step so soon.

I kept reminding myself to do what I could to not mess up what was happening here, whatever it might be.

The car showed up and there were two people in the backseat. Sophie took the front as discussed and I got into the back on the passenger side. The strangers said hello as they slid over to accommodate me, and then, just as we pulled out into the street, they started making out furiously, something I assumed they'd been doing before we hopped into the sedan and were drunk enough to continue in front of two new strangers.

I'd been lucky enough to drunkenly kiss people in public plenty of times, and I understood how if the person is a good enough kisser, the rest of the world around you kind of ceases to exist, so I held no ill will toward these people.

I will say, however, that nothing is worse than the sound of PDA.

Unless, of course, you happen to be one of the participants.

As we drove along, I wondered if they'd been together for a long time or if this was the welcome result of a first night together gone really well that was progressing to something even more intimate when they reached their destination.

It also could've been their third date.

I Thought This Was Worth Sharing

I was delighted when Sophie reached (kind of awkwardly) back through the tiny space between the seats and the doors and took my hand again. I held on, enjoying it for a while, until after a few minutes she slowly pulled away.

I assumed she had to use two hands to type to someone on her phone, but then I realized she was holding her right hand, which was seconds ago clutching mine, over her mouth while she let out a soft burp.

But she seemed mostly fine.

Until we were on the Williamsburg Bridge, when I heard other noises coming from up front that formed a strange symphony with the smacking of lips directly to my left in the backseat.

"Miss, are you OK?" the driver asked with the kind of tone that conveyed he was thinking something like, oh god no, not this shit again.

"I'm fine," she said, but then went back to making guttural sounds.

The driver began to wind down the passenger seat window. You know—just in case.

I, too, put my window down because I figured the more fresh air we got into the car, the better Sophie would feel.

We were halfway across the bridge when she, without much warning aside from some more sickly sounds, leaned out the window and let fly a rather impressive stream of semi-digested daiquiris.

The stream of vomit launched against the wind and flew backward, a pretty hefty amount blowing through my open window and onto my face and torso.

"Oh, no," the driver said flatly with a combination of stoicism and resignation—his acknowledgment and wry acceptance that it was indeed this shit again, another Friday night driving around the drunken idiots of New York City.

I should tell you I don't have a strong stomach.

Far from it.

I'll puke if you look at me the wrong way.

Before high school basketball games, I used to skip the end of warm-ups in favor of running downstairs to the locker room, where I would do a nervous pee-and-puke session in an attempt to get the anxiety demons out.

The couple sitting next to me continued their make-out session, completely oblivious to what had just happened.

This until I leaned my head out of my own window and vomited as well, following suit just like I did when Sophie ordered that first daiquiri.

We were on a sick, sad adventure together, but hey, you know, buy the ticket, take the ride.

With my head out the window, I heard her saying to the driver, "I'm sorry. Oh, god. I'm so fucking sorry."

I let out one last heave, spit, and then settled back into my seat with a heavy sigh, chiming in with my own apologies while the woman sitting next to me, who had finally pulled her lips away from her date, realized (and probably smelled) what was going on.

I THOUGHT THIS WAS WORTH SHARING

She promptly vomited into her date's lap.

It was quite a scene.

Her date did not throw up.

I felt like this was an achievement.

The driver remained stoic.

I found this to be admirable.

But he also showed no mercy. When we finally made it across the bridge, something like eons later, he pulled over to the side of the street at the first opportunity and just started muttering, "Get out. Get out. Get out."

The four of us did, stumbling from our respective doors and assembling as an unruly and dirtied group on the sidewalk. The man from the backseat then began absolutely cracking up. His date chastised him for doing so, but he just yelled, "Only in New York!"

I assumed there were people vomiting in rideshares all over the world at that very moment—that as strange as it was to think, what we were experiencing was really not all that unique. Nothing we ever do is. Something similar to what we'd just been through could easily have been happening in, like, Tulsa.

But I laughed along with him anyway and put my arm around Sophie, who I could feel slightly recoiling for a second before accepting that if she was touching me, she was actually touching mostly her own vomit.

The woman from the Uber vomited more, next to the sidewalk.

Once she gathered herself, we had a bit of a conversation, standing on the side of the road, covered in puke. They actually offered to exchange numbers so we could suss out payments for the inevitable charge from Uber for a thorough car cleaning. But Sophie said she'd started it and she'd take care of it.

Then we went our separate ways. I still wonder if they decided to request another Uber to make their way home or if they took the subway in the state they were in. I kind of wish we *had* exchanged numbers. I'd love to catch up with them and find out what happened with the rest of their night. They seemed like pretty nice people. Maybe if Sophie and I lasted, we could become couple friends with them, and we could laugh every time we got together about how we'd serendipitously and disgustingly met one unexpectedly wild weekend night.

Sophie and I decided to go ahead and walk. Her place was only a few blocks from the bridge, and we thought some fresh air might do us good.

"Do you still want to come over?" she asked.

"Sure," I said. I'd been waiting for her to ask, as I was completely unsure how things would continue after what had just transpired. "But only if you're feeling OK. That was a pretty gnarly experience we just had."

"Well, we'll get you some clean clothes and you can use my shower."

"You have clothing at your apartment that would fit me?"

"We all have exes who leave things."

"I know tonight has been gross on several levels, but wearing your ex-boyfriend's clothes is beyond the limit for me."

I Thought This Was Worth Sharing

"OK, yeah. Makes sense. Maybe you just go home and, if this isn't just some story, if there's more there, we can see each other again soon?"

"Or we just go into a store and I buy some clothes real quick. Maybe a toothbrush."

"You really want to do that?"

"I hate to admit it, but it's not that often that I have a great first date, and I don't want it to end."

"I puked out the window of an Uber. That constitutes great for you?"

"It's been a rough couple of years."

"Fair enough."

We walked into a bodega, where I purchased a toothbrush, a pair of very dad-esque plaid shorts and a T-shirt that said "New York or Nowhere." We also found some semi-fresh limes.

Daiquiri night remained on.

On the walk from the bodega to the liquor store, we held hands again and I told her I loved New York but wasn't sure it was where I'd want to be forever. She said it was fine to not be sure where you wanted to be forever, especially at the stage of life we were both in.

"But it's fine for now," I said, and she responded that "fine for now" is pretty good, that she felt pretty good and sober then, and that we should fix that because the night was young.

I don't know what this says about me exactly, but I found myself becoming even more enamored with Sophie because she was more than ready to rally and consume more of the beverage that had just made her vomit in public. We were gonna play through with the devil we already knew.

So we went back to her place, rum in tow, and took turns showering. (So I guess technically her pants didn't stay on through the entire date.) I changed into my new duds. She made some stellar daiquiris and we had a couple each from a pitcher.

Then we fell asleep on the couch in the middle of *Forgetting Sarah Marshall.*

We were holding hands again when we did.

I woke up happy the next morning despite the kink in my neck from sleeping upright on the couch.

She kissed me goodbye on her building's stoop and asked if she could get me an Uber home.

It was a nice spring day, so I decided to hoof it the two miles or so back to my apartment.

We didn't work out because she still loved someone else.

No harm, no foul. It just happens that way sometimes.

I still love a legit daiquiri, though.

14. Without Her: Ordering Chinese

You used to love to stay in on Friday nights. It's a habit you should maybe get out of, because it made a lot more sense when you had everything you thought you wanted and didn't need to be out there looking for anything.

But you still love it, and that's probably not going to change—not this weekend, anyway.

When you'd stay in with her, you'd order in obnoxious amounts of Chinese food, spread it all out on the coffee table and eat it on the couch while watching one of the shows you'd tacitly agreed to never watch without the other. You know she violated this unwritten rule several times, but you never really minded all that much. Because you did too.

Sometimes one of you would feign surprise at a plot twist during your second viewing, but that was, if we're being brutally honest, far from the worst thing either of you ever faked.

Just because she's not really so much a part of your life anymore doesn't have to change what you like and what you do with your free time.

Just because she doesn't love you anymore doesn't mean you have to do away with the things you loved doing with her.

At least not all of them, anyway, you reason when the hunger first appears during your commute home, the pangs comin' in hot despite the fact that your thoughts of coming home to an empty apartment are making you feel sick to your stomach. It's like part of you wants to eat a dozen fried wontons dipped in ranch dressing (hey, have you ever fucking tried it?) while another part wants to vomit, curl up in the fetal position and never eat anything again.

This doesn't really make sense, but a lot of things don't, especially lately, which is fine.

Everything's fine.

"But what if I want more than fine?" you wonder.

Then you table that thought for another time.

Decision made, you step off the train and stop for a fresh box of Bota Box wine (hey, have you ever fucking tried it?). Arriving home with it in tow, you immediately pour a glass before de-pantsing while simultaneously shuffling over to the couch, where you plop down with a weary-old-man sigh, take out your phone, fire up the food app that sends you a discount code every Friday and get to searching for the components that will make up the large delivery order you hope will help to elevate your mood in some small way.

(And make no mistake—it is a delivery order. Not takeout. Hardly ever takeout. You would always point this out to her. If it were takeout, that'd mean you'd be going to the store to, you know, take it out, bring it home and consume it. Delivery is technically a different thing. She never really conceded this point to you, but didn't exactly argue with you about it either. She'd just let you rant a little bit until you wore yourself out. Thinking of this does nothing except remind you that you were sometimes definitely a prick and that you had a tendency to lose the plot and pay attention to all the wrong details.)

"I hope dim sum goes well with early post-relationship depression," you say out loud to nobody.

The "recently ordered" category at the top of your choices hits you hard in the gut, but not hard enough that you don't persevere in your order. Instead, it opens some new possibilities. It has somehow not occurred to you until now that you're not locked into your usual culinary lineup—that you can add and subtract whatever you want or even start completely from scratch.

That you can try something new.

You attempt to pinpoint when the two of you started ordering the same thing every time, started doing the same things every Friday night (and most other nights), stopped trying to make things more exciting. It takes you two times scrolling through the entire menu without registering you're doing so before you're done with contemplating your culpability in all of this predictability and how much negativity it might have brought to the relationship—how much it might have contributed to its ultimate end.

You put some vegetarian egg foo yung in the cart. It's not that it'd have been frowned upon for you to make such a selection when she was with you exactly, but you never did because it was all about sharing and you knew she wouldn't eat any of what is essentially an omelet smothered in gravy with a side of rice. Many people don't dig egg foo yung, you've found. It's a pretty divisive dish as far as your basic Chinese fare goes, but you've always been of the opinion and palate that is happy when mushroom gravy is added to pretty much anything. (You maybe should have known when she first said she didn't like mushrooms or gravy that things weren't ultimately going to work out.)

You also remember that you can dial it back on the spice scale they give you. She always wanted it as spicy as possible, and you were content with less. (Being content with less in general was more than occasionally a point of contention.) You dial it down from the usual eight to a four.

You could, of course, cut the order in half, but you decide not to do that. You order more food than you can handle. There will be leftovers, plenty of them, but leftovers are key when you plan on spending a weekend in a sedentary and slovenly state. It's not the first weekend since you broke up, but it is the first weekend since she completely left the apartment and the two of you decided you shouldn't communicate in any way, at least not for a while, and you're looking forward to (trying to) rest.

While you wait for the order, you queue up a new show. It's horror. One she would never watch.

The delivery comes swiftly, as always, and it comes with a ridiculous surplus of cutlery. Much more than one person could ever need for what is theoretically one meal. But you're more than happy to toss it

I Thought This Was Worth Sharing

into your junk drawer. You'll need it eventually. Because you don't plan on doing dishes for a while.

You dig in with gusto and something nearing grit, maybe even determination. There's something special about not sharing, at least this one time. You can't make much of a habit of it, though, you think, because you're getting poised to work on a revenge bod. (You call it a revenge bod even though you admittedly have nothing at all to avenge if you're being reasonable about it. The dissolution of the relationship was *mostly* your fault.)

Your diet starts tomorrow, after what you've just consumed makes its way through. There's a good chance you'll be simultaneously shitting and crying sometime in the near future because of your gluttony and your inability to avoid thinking about her at the most random times, like when you're on the commode.

But for now things feel OK. And you're trying to get better with the "for now," to live more in the moment than maybe you ever have before.

You have more than your fill and put the rest in the refrigerator.

Then you go to the finishing ritual: the opening of the fortune cookie.

But the delivery came with two.

You wonder which one is meant for you.

Scott Muska

15. Selected Excerpts From Dating Application Cover Letters

1. I realize that I may not have experience commensurate with the requirements you have posted for this role, but I am still somehow confident I could make you very happy if you just took a seemingly random leap of faith and gave me a chance.

2. I hope this message finds you well. I have already applied for your potential affection via a right swipe on Bumble, but figured it might not hurt to follow up here on Hinge. I hope you will see this pursuit on multiple platforms as enthusiasm and not over-eagerness.

3. I'll be the first to admit that I have zero experience with polyamory but am the kind of go-getter who will try everything once. I'm also a team player and work well with others.

4. Thank you so much in advance for taking the time to read my message. I know you probably receive many that are similar in several ways to this one, but I hope it, along with my bio and profile pictures, will pique your interest enough to spark a conversation and maybe at some point an informal in-person meeting.

5. I can't say I was looking to enter singledom and begin seeking a new significant other so soon, as I have just been let go from my most recent situation and am honestly still more than a little sad about it, but this seems like it could be a great opportunity—one that could potentially change my life forever and hopefully for the better, along with, well, yours. The dissolution of my aforementioned relationship was amicable since both of us acknowledged that neither of us had for some time been particularly diligent in executing our roles as previously understood and initially expected. In fact, it went on for much longer than necessary, but I had, to be honest, been waiting for some time for my former "other half" (her term, not mine) to broach the topic, as I am not great with confrontation. (In fact, I will list this as one of my greatest weaknesses if ever you ask.)

6. I would prefer full-time for this position, as I have been looking (almost desperately) for as much for the better part of a decade and would enjoy the benefits that come with such a role, but understand that nonexclusivity may make the most sense, especially initially, as a trial period of sorts. I'd be more than willing to undergo a semiformal evaluation after about one fiscal quarter, if that would be agreeable, though I will also cede that I am in no real rush regarding either a timeline or an official title.

7. If you take a look at my attached dating résumé, you will see that I have hopped around a decent amount and have not in the past decade held any position for much longer than a year, but I promise I can explain my reasons for leaving or being dismissed from any of

I Thought This Was Worth Sharing

these positions and am confident I have learned from each experience.

8. My dear friend Brenda has referred me to this position after first mentioning a few months ago that it might soon become available and that I might be a great fit. Apologies if I'm reaching out too soon, and I acknowledge it's always kind of weird when your friends set you up because then those friends hear every detail from both sides when things inevitably go wrong, but dang it all to heck, let's give it a shot anyway! If you agree that we should, you can reach me at any time of day or night at this email address. I sincerely hope to hear from you.

9. My coworker Steven previously occupied this position. You may or may not recall that we met when he brought you to a party once. Since he has since resigned—something I'm told he did without warning—I would love the opportunity to throw my hat in the ring as a potential replacement. When you're ready, of course. Is it weird to try to date one of your work friend's exes? Sure. But in my opinion, what's weirder is his decision to terminate your relationship.

Scott Muska

16. Free Stuff: Three-pack (One Opened) of Mrs. Meyers's Clean Day Hand Soap, Geranium Scent

I thought I'd ordered the lavender. So it was a kick in the dick when I opened the Amazon box to find I'd actually purchased geranium. I looked up my order history to ensure that there hadn't been some sort of mistake on the shipping front and found that, as usual, the blame could be directed nowhere other than at myself. I guess that'll teach me to do my online shopping after having several too many spiked seltzers—though I do take some comfort in the notion that my drunken mistakes can be turned into learning experiences. Because, of course, this is about more than soap. The geranium scent is the one my ex-girlfriend stocked in her bathroom. I used it from time to time and grew very fond of it because it lingered on her, mixed with a bouquet of other scents, all of which now give me flashbacks to the good times I can't help but miss before sending me into a rapid spiral regarding my romantic failures from the relationship's promising beginning to its abrupt end. Using that soap is certainly not going to help me wash away my nostalgia. Of this I am certain. I have no interest in conducting some sort of exposure therapy experiment with the product. I'd rather be rid of it.

A note: One of the containers is opened and has been gently used, as I didn't fully register that the soap was a scent that would trigger me until I pumped a couple of dollops onto my hands after dicing up several onions, and no, I wasn't crying; you were crying. If you don't want that one, I get it. But if you do, more power to you. Just let me know where you live and whether you want the two or three containers, and I'll go ahead and ship 'em to you gratis. I see no reason to completely waste them, you know? I mean, I thought briefly about sending them to her, but we're no longer in contact. I don't know her address, and I feel like making such a move anyway would not be greeted with much warmth—understandably so, to say the least. I operate under the assumption that she, more than justifiably, may want to forget about me more than I want to forget about her or, more aptly, the way I treated her. She was just fine.

But seriously. It's really good soap.

form a Dating Exit Interview
17. Questions From a Dating Exit Interview

Thank you for coming in today! Have a seat. Yes, next to the replica of the leg lamp from *A Christmas Story*. I like to leave it up year-round because it does emanate a soft, comforting light.

How's your morning been? Oh, mine? Yes, fine. Getting better and stronger every day. Or at least that's a lie I tell my therapist. Ha.

Anyway.

I suppose we'd better get into it.

What made you decide to leave this position so quickly, even before we reached our 90-day review—that pivotal point in a relationship? I acknowledge there may be one single thing, or a laundry list of things. After thinking about this for a long while, I have decided that I'd prefer if you were honest with me and as detailed as possible. Make it hurt. The knowing is, I think, better than not knowing in this scenario because I have a tendency to wonder, and when I wonder, my mind wanders to places that are, more often than not, much worse than the reality. If I did fuck up as badly as my thoughts will undoubtedly make me believe I did, it's best to know for sure so I can learn from my mistakes and truly improve by the next time I hit reset and start over.

If I feel like I like someone, I feel as though I should act like I like that person. I'm told this is not at all the way to go about it—that it's some kind of game. So can I ask, did the rather immediate expression of my genuine burgeoning interest in you actually serve to drive you away? If so, how might I avoid such a situation in the future? Would it help to passively act like I don't like a person in hopes it will make me more appealing? If so, do you find it odd that such counterintuitive things seem to work so well?

Did I try way too hard to make you laugh? And then laugh heartily at my own jokes even though they were not funny? (Goddammit. I swore I was going to stop doing that.)

Was there someone else? I get that this happens and is completely normal, especially since we never had any discussion about exclusivity, but I always wonder if it's better to lose out to someone instead of just flat-out losing to my own damn self. If so, who were they? I'd like to use search engines to do my own in-depth comparative analysis.

Do you wish I had taken the initiative to end things to make it easier on you? Did it seem as though I was content to keep dragging things out in hopes you would ghost or finally pull the proverbial plug so I could pretend to be bitter about it? Did you at any point begin to suspect that

I THOUGHT THIS WAS WORTH SHARING

I suspected you were fading? Do you believe I'm asking some of these questions because I am, in fact, bitter?

What were the most important factors, facets and traits in your decision to take on a new suitor (if indeed you have done so)? Benefits? Time off? Affluence? Sexual prowess? Confidence? What does he offer that I did not or was incapable of providing?

What, if anything, could I do to get you to stay? Please keep in mind my current budgetary restraints.

Were you ever truly sexually satisfied, or did you fake it? Or did you not even attempt to fake it and I am just really not at all as intuitive or dialed in as I thought I might be?

Were there any unforeseen challenges that you had to contend with when it came to not only dating me specifically but putting up with me in general? Would you like me to rattle off my perceived shortcomings and inadequacies, and you simply nod in the negative or the affirmative?

I am not by any means saying we were in love, but I also won't say I didn't have hopes that it would ultimately go in that direction. So, why do you think love, like the opposite of weight, is so easy to lose but difficult to find?

Scott Muska

I THOUGHT THIS WAS WORTH SHARING

18. Quiz: Text From Someone I'm Dating or From My Food Delivery Driver?

1. "Are you sure you live here?"

2. "I've been waiting for a very long time."

3. "If I go any faster, it could endanger myself and others."

4. "I hope you're saving some of that for tomorrow."

5. "I'm pretty sure there's only one entrance where I'm allowed."

6. "Do you think you'll ever be ready to try something new?"

7. "I pretty much always come early. Maybe I go too fast."

8. "Well, it smells like pepperoni."

9. "You can have it all."

10. "The quicker I get there, the hotter it is."

11. "No. That is absolutely not what you said you wanted. I have it in writing right here."

12. "Look, I'll give it to someone else if you don't want it."

13. "I never asked for this."

14. "Send it back if you want."

15. "I slipped on the way in."

16. "It spilled everywhere."

17. "After this, I'm finished for the night."

18. "You're seriously alone?"

19. "You should know your voicemail isn't set up."

20. "If I don't hear from you, I'm leaving in five minutes."

21. "Did you seriously fall asleep on me again?"

22. "I'm not asking you to meet me halfway."

23. "I can't believe it took 45 minutes."

I THOUGHT THIS WAS WORTH SHARING

24. "I feel like anyone would have a hard time finding it."

25. "Sorry. It's too late."

Food delivery driver: 1, 2, 3, 4, 5, 6, 7, 8, 9, 10, 11, 12, 13, 14, 15, 16, 17, 18, 19, 20, 21, 22, 23, 24 and 25.

Someone I'm dating: None.

Scott Muska

19. When You Know They're Fading

You wake up hours before your alarm is set to go off, eager, anxious and maybe even a little optimistic. There's the potential that overnight, while you have been restlessly drifting in and out of consciousness, things have somehow changed, that the pendulum has swung back in what you would call your favor—and they have decided to rekindle a conversation that on their end has become mostly ashes and a few embers left (you think) intentionally glowing.

It's kind of counterintuitive (not to mention potentially detrimental to overall mental health), but there's a pretty direct correlation between how frequently you check your phone and their gradual lapse in communication.

The less they text, the more you hope they will—and the more you try to will it into existence.

You know this is not at all the way it should be. Not if things are going in the direction you hoped for.

When you check there are, not surprisingly, but sadly, no pertinent phone notifications.

You return your head to your pillow and close your eyes, though you know without a doubt that you're not falling back asleep in the two hours and change you have left before you have to get out of bed and attempt to make your way through a day of work that will be rife with distraction as you continuously check your phone even though it hasn't even buzzed.

You know now that fatigue will be added to the mix, which is frustrating but unavoidable.

Your thoughts during these early morning hours are often a loop of something sort of like this: The bottom fell out, buddy. Now it's time to question what you did or did not do to get to this point, which is a definite lapse in communication that will probably endure. Bet you can't wait to randomly think about this person and concoct theories about what you may have done wrong every so often over the next few weeks or months or maybe, in some cases, years, depending on your level of sensitivity at the moment and your level of interest in this person.

"Why am I like this?" you say out loud to a dark, empty room.

***

"Things are really going great," you told your friends, and you earnestly believed it because you had no real reason to think otherwise.

I Thought This Was Worth Sharing

You even told your mom you met someone new—something you're often hesitant to do because she gets a little too excited for you about these things, though her sympathy is always welcomed in the event that shit goes south.

You may have jumped the gun on that one—got overeager, as you have been known to do.

But by this point you'd been talking with them nearly constantly, sending several messages back and forth daily, getting together a couple of times a week, give or take, the windows of opportunity to do so dictated by busy schedules. You've been sending each other all kinds of things, like links to Bon Iver's cover of "I Can't Make You Love Me," which they countered with a clip of Dashboard Confessional singing a surprisingly somewhat beautiful version of a Justin Bieber song. There have even been pep talks after she confided in you that she was beginning to lament completely selling out career-wise. (It was easy to provide some hopefully comforting words because you had long since done the same thing.)

You tried not to get too excited about all this, especially not so soon, but figured if you could control what you got excited about, you'd make it so you got excited about work or working out or eating healthy or taxes or socializing or all kinds of other things you really don't ever feel much like doing.

Maybe you should have tried harder, because before too long the communication became less frequent and more sparse. Texts went from eloquent and enthusiastic to terse and trite. They were petering out until communication became sporadic at best, your asks to hang out met with vague reasons they were unavailable.

But they hadn't disappeared, not completely.

***

It dawns on you, or you finally admit what you've been thinking for some time, while you're lying in bed that morning: They're doing a Slow Fade—slow enough that you can't really call them out on it without their calling you overbearing or crazy.

It is, honestly, a pretty solid move.

You know this because you've done it to others, so you kick yourself under the comforter for not having figured it out sooner. It somehow seemed less harsh, less reprehensible, more justified when you did it to someone else. Funny how that works, isn't it? You realize this, too, feel pretty terrible about it and add it to the scroll of things to beat yourself up about now and for the foreseeable future.

You can't know what this person is thinking, what's going on in their life. Could be all kinds of things. You have had plenty of reasons for doing in the past what they're doing now. None of them are particularly justifiable or even defensible when the ethical alternative to the Slow Fade is one simple text saying you don't think things are going to work out and best of luck in all your future endeavors, but sometimes people go through shit. Sometimes people simply lose interest. Or they meet someone else. Could be any number of variables or a combination of them, really.

But you assume they're hoping you'll get the hint, that you'll let them avoid a slightly difficult conversation they don't want to have.

Part of you is tempted to just let this happen because you may be better off not knowing how and when you fucked up, if you did indeed fuck up.

I Thought This Was Worth Sharing

You've always been one to worry about negative feedback.

Sometimes it's better to not know where you fell short, what they may think is wrong with you, why you're not compatible and why things simply aren't going to go the way you hoped they would.

Sometimes it's easier to go your separate ways.

Sometimes it's actually better to vanish into thin air than to explain oneself.

But still, you won't let them off easy.

You text, "Will I ever see you again?"

Then you put your phone on Do Not Disturb, bust out your weighted blanket and try to rest for a while.

Scott Muska

20. Text Messages You Should Probably Not Send As a First Date Follow-Up

Thank you so much for coming out with me tonight. Your company is like chicken soup for the lonely male soul!

Just talked to my best friend and told him to get to work on a Best Man speech!

Tonight was great. I felt like we really connected. I know it's early to say this, but you're really helping me get over my ex. At first I was pretty torn up about it, but now I honestly can't wait until she moves out!

I think I'm tumbling into like with you.

I miss you already.

I just texted my mom about you, and she says she can't wait to meet you, hopefully someday soon!

I'm too excited to go to sleep, so instead I'm going to make you a chapbook of handwritten haiku.

Hey, I know we just went out tonight, but what are you up to tomorrow and, like, forever?

I know there are so many better people out there than me in this city, but I could really love you well if you would deem me worthy of doing so!

We should probably run away together.

You know how, during our date, I kept saying you looked like someone I knew, maybe someone famous, but I wasn't able to put my finger on who? It just came to me: one of my favorite porn actors!

I think you might be the one.

I have never felt a connection like this before.

Normally I wouldn't text so soon for a second date, but my friend is a bookie, a bunch of dudes have taken action on the over/under of how long this courtship might last and they won't stop bothering me about it, so would you like to go out with me again sometime in the near future?

Maybe we should go out and do karaoke sometime. I'll sing the Peter Gabriel version of "The Book of Love." My ex used to love that song. God, I miss her so much sometimes.

I love you.

21. Losing My Lip Balm

"This morning I misplaced a tube of lip balm. We've all been there. Many of us many times. I'm not unique in this. Doesn't mean I'm not alone in it. This loss will likely stay with me even longer than the balm itself did. When I lose something, especially in a way I had some semblance of control and responsibility over, I am eventually fully conscious to an intense degree, and to a fault, of the void it left. And that feeling of absence tends to endure for a longer stretch than the time whatever it was that is now gone spent making me feel closer to whole. This tube of balm was with me through some tough, great, exciting and nearly unbearable times, which to me counts for something significant, worth remembering and lamenting. It was a pomegranate-flavored one from Burt's Bees, no different or not much more so than the one of several you've had in your pocket or your purse or somewhere on your person through the years, and it had probably done nothing more for me than something like it has probably done for you. I bet you've even lost at least one or two, if not several, or that you might be the kind of person that has a constant rotation of them situated pretty much everywhere, so you're never really left without. But to me, this one was extremely special. Of course it wasn't at all lost on me that there was some sort of end in sight. I knew it from the start, or even before the start—I mean, nothing is indefinite, really; forever is just a construct—but I hoped that end wouldn't come so unexpectedly, that I wouldn't make the mistake that sent it away to wherever it is now. I thought I'd see it through to empty barrel, to its reasonable conclusion, when things had run their course for better or worse. A hole in my pocket might have been a factor. Or maybe something distracted me, for a minute there I lost myself, and I put it someplace different than usual and then didn't know where to even start looking once I finally did find myself again. I don't know. Probably never will. And I have to somehow square with that, accept complete culpability. But anyway, I think it's gone for good now, as they say, though I never understood that phrase. Should probably be gone for bad, if you really think about it. At least in some cases. All I know is that now I have to go out and try to find some more lip balm. Or the cracks are going to widen. I might not be able to find one as great as what I had and lost, but it's not coming back, so that's no reason to stop searching."

"Dude. Are you sure you're talking about ChapStick?"

22: Reading in Bed, Forever Ago

We were together, and I can't forget the rest.

She came to visit me in Bushwick after a night spent at her place back home over the holidays. There had been lead-up to that night, a lot of texting after we connected on social media years after going to the same high school together and never really interacting. We'd gotten drinks near her apartment in a smaller city not far from where we would always be from, and she took me to her apartment with her, said she didn't expect me to drive back to my parents' place.

She made her cat stay out of the bedroom because of my allergies. I was happy about that, but I assume the cat was not. I have this notion that cats are more often unhappy than not—but I may look at them only as generally ornery because my aforementioned allergies generate an involuntarily negative perception. And I realize it's unfair to make such a blanket statement because cats' attitudes are based on many different things, like where and how they grew up and their own general ingrained temperament. Kind of like how I'm a Scorpio but bristle when people assume they know anything about me and who I inherently am because I was born on a certain day. I am not magically adept at sex because I was born on November 6, for example. Wish I was, but them's the breaks.

Getting back to the whole visiting-me thing.

She was in town for work and decided to make a weekend of it. She would stay even though she hated the trains. Her telling me that is what it took for me to finally download a rideshare app. A lot happened in the span of about two days.

We kissed. I think I fell in love, something that can be easy to do. She told me her face went numb and gave me a high-five. I didn't tell her I didn't come, couldn't make it happen, mostly because of the meds, though booze played a part, like it so often does. Didn't get into the whole thing about how sometimes I'm sick and sad and haven't yet figured out how not to let it affect how I treat and interact with other people, including and especially the ones I love, the ones who get close. She did tell me she didn't want kids, no matter what, and would stay with the IUD indefinitely. It made me think about whether I wanted children or not, though it was all so abstract. I had just left one professional thing and was looking for where my next dose of nearly unaffordable health care coverage was going to come from. I couldn't even take care of myself, let alone someone else.

We ate a lot, stayed in, and said we should go out and do something but instead just kept each other company.

I Thought This Was Worth Sharing

There was this string of moments I'll always remember and wish I didn't, when we laid in my bed and just read silently next to each other for the better part of an hour. Could've been even longer. I thought maybe that was something I could enjoy doing with her every day, or at least on leisurely weekends, and wondered why comfortable silence so often seemed so elusive.

She left in fear on Sunday night via a train to the airport. Said she could never live in New York, no matter what, because of, among other things, the whole fear of trains—dubbed *Eisenbahnangst* by, of course, Freud.

But who really can live in New York?

(Funny, though, she lives there now. And I do not. Things change, right? So do people. Wonder where she now stands on the whole having kids thing. I tell myself I don't really care, but I'm writing this, so clearly I do, right?)

I clung to that weekend for a long time, even when and especially after she had begun to fade, did that thing where she was less communicative to a point you knew something was off, but not to the point where you could call her out on it without her being able to say you were overreacting.

If you don't know what I'm talking about, good.

She said she was moving to Los Angeles but didn't.

She never even told me she didn't want to pursue taking it further. Instead she just kind of stopped talking to me altogether except for the one time a year later when she was visiting again without having told me and texted me to see what I was doing—because her host was boring her.

I've drunkenly texted her several times, asking why I wasn't good enough, but have gotten no reply. Yes, I am embarrassed for having done this. No, I do not really want an answer.

I sometimes wish that weekend had never happened, but at the same time, I'm glad that while I didn't find what I was looking for, it helped me figure out what I wasn't.

It's been five years of reading alone.

And I hate to say it, but I still wonder what she's reading.

ine
23. Reasons They Can't (or Don't Want to) Sleep Over

They're too excited about the fact that they've just had sex with a beautiful person like you and know they won't be able to sleep, so instead they feel they must walk (or frolic) all the way home, no matter how far that is, while they listen to Hall & Oates' "You Make My Dreams" on repeat.

They have to go home and let their (stuffed) dog out.

They're too shy to blow up your bathroom until you've been together for at least one fiscal quarter.

When sleeping in unfamiliar places, they have a tendency to sleepwalk and sometimes sleep eat, and don't want to wake up in your basement communal laundry room or something, covered in mayonnaise and peanut butter, which has maybe happened before.

They're a little bit worried there are monsters under your bed or in your closet and how are they supposed to know for sure that there aren't unless they look, which might freak you out? Sure, they could wait until you go to the bathroom or something, but as they've learned in the past, there's no guarantee this will happen and they'll be stuck there all night vaguely fearing for their own life. Even though they know the likelihood is slim to literally impossible, there's still that flicker of doubt, and that flicker of doubt can be extremely powerful.

Because they have a rule: No sleepovers on school nights. They know they won't sleep too well with other people outside of their familiar bed and its surroundings, and while they did have a great time with you, they aren't ready to sacrifice a needed night's rest for a prolonged cuddle session followed by their tossing and turning and feeling bad not only because they're awake, but because they're keeping you awake as well. Please don't be too offended by this. If they could sleep anywhere with anyone, they surely would, and they're not leaving in an attempt to make you feel anything negative. If you had a good time and want to see them again, maybe give it another go on the weekend, when neither of you has to wake up early the next morning.

They begin their day, without fail, with a very particular routine that includes certain mandatories like weeping in the shower as they think about the hours ahead of them, practicing the Wim Hof Method or some type of meditation to quell the deep-chested sobs, preparing a shake or omelet, etc.

They're disappointed in their performance and would like to retreat home in shame to chastise themselves while reviewing their internal recording of the previous proceedings for spots where they might improve if ever they get another shot.

They talk in their sleep and are afraid of what you might hear.

I Thought This Was Worth Sharing

They have medicine at home that they have to take either tonight or tomorrow morning, or else there are going to be negative consequences.

The morning commute from your apartment to their workplace would be insane, and they also do not feel like wearing the same outfit from the previous day because then people might notice and inquire about their personal business, and they like to keep that detached from their work life the best they can.

They have to get home to the family they haven't told you about.

They just straight-up don't want to, and part of being single in the first place is doing whatever you want when you want.

They have a curfew.

They're deathly allergic to your cat but don't want to tell you because they don't want to offend either you or the cat.

They promised their roommate they would be home in time to tell them a bedtime story.

They can only sleep in a very specific atmosphere, with the temperature at 68 degrees or lower and both a fan roaring and a white noise machine playing simulated rain sounds.

They believe that sleeping in a stranger's bed is more intimate than being sexually intimate with them and they're not yet ready for that level of intimacy, which is weird to think about, but just because something is weird doesn't mean it isn't true.

Scott Muska

24. Some Potential Reasons Why They Ghosted You

They're, like, totally swamped at work.

They heard you the other night on your third date when you drunkenly mumbled, "I think I love you" under your breath.

They're just totally not ready to date right now even though they thought they were when they decided to fire up the dating apps again. Sometimes you want to do something and you just can't.

You habitually wear socks during sex and you're not very good at boning to begin with. Your performance is subpar at best. Too much tongue in the kissing, not enough tongue in the oral, etc.

You were a pawn to help them get their ex back.

They met someone better than you (who may actually be the love of their life) and would prefer slowly making their way out of your life to actually revealing this to you, because in the past people have over-reacted in strange and sometimes unsettling ways to finding out that they weren't viewed, in the eyes of someone they've been attempting to court, as the most viable of potential partners.

They found out about the hookers.

They checked out your Instagram and noticed the correlation between your body weight fluctuation and whether or not you are actively look-ing for a relationship or comfortably in a committed one, and they've decided to get out before you get into gains mode.

They've justified in their mind (and potentially justifiably so, depend-ing on several variables and their own personal ethical code) that they don't really owe you anything at all—including an explanation of why they no longer want you to be a part of their life.

They decided that multitasking is stupid and that they wouldn't breathe and text you at the same time anymore, and they're a slow typist with subpar lung capacity.

They know what you did last summer.

You came on way too strongly way too quickly and freaked them out.

They read the morning briefing of current events in the country and, in reaction, whipped their phone across the room, where it shattered against the beautiful exposed brick they have in their apartment. They have not been diligent with their cloud data backups and so have found

I Thought This Was Worth Sharing

themselves unable to recover your contact information, and they also happen to be dismal at using Google.

They were a figment of your imagination. In fact, none of this is real.

They have become a zombie.

They have experienced the calling of the cloth and have felt compelled to become either a nun or a priest.

You fucked up the whole "your" and "you're" thing one too goddamn many times.

They have been married this whole time and their spouse found out, so they had to cut ties immediately and without notice with you and anyone else they have been seeing. (How did their spouse find out? Well, it could've happened in any number of ways, including said spouse coming across their partner's online dating profile—which, when brought up, started an argument where they were both questioning why the other was on a dating app, the result being the revelation that they have both been cheating and should maybe explore ethical nonmonogamy or something.)

You always have coffee breath.

You front-loaded everything interesting about yourself and quickly became insufferably boring.

Because shit happens.

Because everybody's doing it and we pretty much all have at one time or another. It's not always the worst way to end things.

Scott Muska

ACKNOWLEDGMENTS

Thanks to Paul Shirley, Dan Moore, Kay Bolden, Tre Loadholt and all the other writers, editors and friends who have helped me become better at what I do, and who have helped me get my work seen.

Thanks to anyone who has ever read any of my stuff and said a nice word or two about it.

Thank you above all else to my Mom and Dad, who taught me to love reading at a young age, and who have provided unwavering support of my writing ever since.

Scott Muska

ABOUT THE AUTHOR

Scott Muska writes stories, essays, poems and ads. This is his first book. He lives in Chicago.

Made in the USA
Columbia, SC
19 June 2022

61934841R00068